2020

The year that

changed the world

Naomi Lumutenga

Illustrated by Taaya Griffith

Contents

Introduction

2020 has been a year that has forced us to slam the brakes on for life as we (thought we) knew it; just like that, bang! Starting with the tragic death of basketball legend Kobe Bryant, his daughter Gianna and seven other people in a helicopter crash on January 26th, momentous events continued to unfold that triggered the need to record them for future generations.

On 31st January, the United Kingdom formally left the European Union, after forty-seven years of membership. The UK's exit brought an end to the prolonged bruising political wrangles that had led to a referendum won by the Leave side, and seen off two Conservative Party Prime Ministers (David Cameron and Teresa May); in came the third, Boris Johnson, promising to 'Get Brexit Done'. While the rest of the world watched European events curiously, evaluating how Brexit would impact them, it was the underlying health issues emerging from China that would soon make everyone stop and take note

In December 2019, health officials in Wuhan, China, had confirmed that they were monitoring a virus that had infected dozens of people. The Chinese government responded by placing Wuhan, a city with eleven million people, and surrounding areas, under quarantine. What started off as an epidemic in China soon spread to Europe and, by mid-March, the death toll from the novel virus in Italy had surpassed that in China. The ease of travel that has reduced the world to a global village, enabled the novel coronavirus to spread like an invisible fire across the world. In the absence of a unified global response, individual governments devised de-facto quarantines of variable strictness, culminating in a global shutdown.

Suddenly, it did not matter what make of car, or whether one owned a private jet, we all had to 'stay at home'. The world's busiest airports and highways were empty and eerily silent. Soon wild animals were spotted in cities. Mega global events, such as the Tokyo Olympics, were cancelled. Schools had to come up with alternative plans for teaching and conducting public exams. Homes became classrooms (and offices) and parents became their children's teachers, overnight. We queued up outside and inside supermarkets and fought over hand sanitiser, toilet rolls, pasta, and flour. We discovered how to socialise and work, remotely. We mastered the art of avoiding human contact, sometimes at the risk of getting run over by a car. City dwellers discovered the joy of birdsongs. We craved the opportunity to hug our loved ones. We learned new vocabulary, which will feature later.

For the British Royal Family, 2020 will be remembered as the year when the Queen's grandson Prince Harry, his American wife Meghan and their son, Archie, swapped the pomp of castles, palaces and royal regalia with a new life in the USA.

2020 has been the year when governments found money trees; they cushioned private businesses, paid salaries, and temporarily housed the homeless! It has been the year when the previously unknown virus rattled royalty and some of the most protected and powerful political leaders. As illustrated here, 2020 is a year that changed the world.

This book is intended to capture some of those memories for future reference; it is non-judgemental and endeavours to show positive green shoots peering through challenging times. It is not exhaustive because; 1) it was compiled before the end of the year and, 2) it was intended to be a general snapshot, at the time of writing. Extra effort has been made to include activities that are worthy of celebration but may not be deemed newsworthy. The multi-dimensional nature of the events means that detailed analyses will require specialist research in respective areas of interest.

DEDICATION

This book is dedicated to those who did extraordinary things to help others: campaigns to change policy (for example, footballer Marcus Rashford), fundraising (especially inspirational centurions), key workers or essential workers and first responders, media, charitable organisations, scientific researchers, neighbours, individual community volunteers and children who made abrupt adjustments to their lives. We think of the impact of the sudden events, on the mental health of surviving key workers, who risked their lives to keep us safe. We honour memories of those who lost their lives while helping others, during the pandemic and think of their families and friends.

The final dedication is to my beloved mother, Feriktas Karen Muzaki Watasa (1935-2020), whose inspiring spirit always loves, teaches, and asks the question, 'What have you done today, to make the world a better place?'

New words created and old words redefined by 2020

Asymptomatic
a person who is infected with COVID-19 but shows no symptoms

Blursday
when one loses track of time because of lockdown disorientation

Bubble
a group of people with whom one can interact safely

Covidiot
Someone who ignores government and public health guidelines.

Covideo party
A party or social event held via video

Circuit break
A UK government initiative that is a short, sharp period of tightened restrictions for everyone to halt the spread of coronavirus.

Doom scrolling
A new habit of scrolling through web-pages, searching for the latest COVID-19 news that then makes us miserable.

Drive-thru funerals
When a priest could stand by a corridor at a funeral home to bless each hearse in quick succession, especially in Spain and Italy, during the peak of the pandemic.

Eat-out to Help-out
A scheme by the British Government, to help keep restaurants in business by encouraging people to eat out, on a government subsidy of 50% of the bill, or up to £10.

Face covering
A mask or scarf worn over the nose and mouth to reduce the spread of the coronavirus.

Furlough
To grant paid leave of absence to an employee; this was adopted as many employers were instructed to shut down during the pandemic.

Hybrid classes
A mixture of online with physical teaching and learning.

Lockdown
A set of national or regional restrictions to movement of people, opening of businesses and public areas, to contain and control the spread of the coronavirus.

New normal
The collective description of new behaviours and activities, such as stepping out of the way from an oncoming person, virtual interactions, not socialising or visiting family, interacting with a physician online only.

PPE (Personal Protection Equipment)
Protective equipment that all frontline workers needed, while attending to COVID-19 infected people.

Quarantine
Mandatory isolation in designated areas, for fourteen days.

Revenge-buying
Spike in sales as shoppers spend money saved during lockdown.

Rona
Short form (or nickname) for coronavirus

R1, R2...
Denotes the rate at which infections spread; for example, R2 means that one infected person can infect two others.

'Scientific' wedding/funeral
Coined by Ugandan President Museveni to describe much scaled-down weddings and funerals during the pandemic (usually 800-2,000 participants).

Self-isolation
When one has been in contact with an infected person or presents with possible symptoms of COVID-19 and remains indoors, with no physical contacts, for fourteen days.

Shielding or Shelter in place
People deemed most at risk of becoming seriously ill from the new coronavirus, advised to stay indoors and have no contact with anyone outside their home, until given the all-clear or told to evacuate.

Social distancing
To keep two metres (six feet) away from another person

Super-spreader
A highly contagious person (in this case) infected with COVID-19.

Take-a-knee
To kneel during the national anthem as a form of protest; initiated by NFL player Colin Kaepernick, it became a global symbol of support for the Black Lives Matter movement.

WFH (Working from Home)
All people (apart from key workers or first responders and other designated persons) devised ways of getting their work done, without leaving their homes.

Zoombombing
Hijacking or hacking into a Zoom event

Zooming
Virtual interaction using Zoom

TRANSPORT NODES AND ROUTES

The air travel tailspin

Various sources indicate that on an ordinary day there are 150,000 - 180,000 aircrafts in the sky; they include commercial and small aeroplanes, private jets, and helicopters. The abrupt stop to international flights, to control the spread of the coronavirus, hit the global airline industry like a meteorite! Starting with Asia, followed by Europe and North America, air traffic fell by 70 - 90%; Dubai International Airport suspended all passenger flights, for two weeks, from March 25th. By the end of July 2020 global airlines had lost about US $880 billion.

The world's busiest passenger airport, Harts-field-Jackson, Atlanta (USA), which ordinarily handles over 2,600 flights a day dropped to 1,200 (mostly empty) flights in mid-April. By mid-March it had shut three of its five runaways and converted them into parking lots for over 600 grounded aircrafts. Grounded aircrafts became a new phenomenon across the world's busiest airports.

Elsewhere, Los Angeles air traffic fell by 95%, London Heathrow by 90%, 85% in New Zealand, Sydney Airport (AUS) 97%.

Ghost City Centres and Subways

In compliance with the 'stay at home, save lives' appeal from leaders all over the world, global megacities became ghost spaces. Popular shopping centres, like London's historic Oxford Street, long considered Europe's busiest shopping street (having an estimated 500,000 visitors daily) with its attractive iconic shops like Selfridges, House of Fraser, John Lewis, HMV and the usually crowded Soho and Covent Garden areas were deserted. New York's elegant and expensive Fifth Avenue had the odd motorist and dogwalker; all the high-end mega stores, like Armani, Abercrombie & Finch, Apple Store, Bergdorf, Louis Vuitton, and many others were closed. In Paris, the most recognisable landmark, the Eiffel Tower, was closed, for three months, the first time the tower was closed since WWII. In India, the must-visit Taj Mahal on the Yamuna River in Uttar Pradesh was closed and only partially re-opened in September, under new restrictions, to 5,000 people (compared to 70,000 prior to C-19 closure) daily.

Abrupt closures accelerated or triggered the exit of some household store names and airlines. In USA, the once-upon-a-time must visit stores, like Macy's and JC Penny, will cease trading by the end of 2020. Others include Pier 1 Imports, Tuesday Morning, Bed Bath & Beyond, and GameStop; altogether, over 13,000 well-known businesses were earmarked for closure, by mid-August. British shoppers will no longer find the imposing Debenhams, synonymous with high streets in large cities; other victims of 2020 include Harvey's Furniture, TM Lewin (shirts and ties), Bertram Books, JD Sports, Monsoon, Victoria's Secrets, Cath Kidston, and Laura Ashley. Global airlines that have gone out of business (or expected to go) include South African Airways (along with its subsidiary South African Express); German Wings, SunExpress and German Airways (Germany); Nantucket Express, Trans States Airlines, Compass Airlines, Ravn, and Miami Air International (USA); LEVEL Europe (Austria); CityJet (France); NokScoot (Thailand); Tigerair Australia (a subsidiary of Virgin Australia) and Flybe (UK). These businesses were large employers and their exit (combined with the restructuring for survivors) is catastrophic, in terms of employment and impact on families and dependent small businesses.

However, while actual data will take time to collect and analyse, anecdotal evidence indicates unexpected alternative outcomes. The Guardian (April 3rd 2020) reported that empty streets 'have already resulted in big drops in air pollution, which is likely to reduce early deaths from lung and heart conditions. Traffic deaths and injuries are near certain to have fallen, but data is not yet available. Noise pollution, which is also known to have adverse effects on human health, is down, and the quieter streets have encouraged wildlife to venture into some towns.'

It is reasonable to assume that this improvement in air quality has been replicated around the world.

Wildlife

Another unexpected spectacle is that of wildlife having a wild time in cities and popular recreational centres. In Chile, pumas were spotted prowling the streets of downtown Santiago. In Italy, dolphins showed up in untypically calm waters in the harbour of Trieste; while the stoppage of motorised boats transporting tourists up and down the canals in Venice gave way to clear water and some residents were surprised to see seaweed and shoals of fish. A herd of buffalo were spotted strolling along an empty highway in New Delhi, India, on 8th April. A deer took its turn across a pedestrian crossing in Nara, Japan, on 19th March. Residents were treated to a herd of fallow deer grazing on the lawns in front of a housing estate in Harold Hill in East London (UK) on 4th April. In South Africa, penguins discovered and calmly waddled through the streets of Simonstown, near Cape Town; kudu were spotted nibbling the suburban lawns near Pretoria and, near Kruger National Park there was an unusual alliance of lions-hyenas-impalas-wild dogs relaxing in the nearby Skukuza Golf Course.

EDUCATION SYSTEMS

Homeschooling

Reference to 'education' in this context is confined to 'schooling' systems that governments have created to deliver approved curricula, in institutions, with measurable outcomes. By the end of March, virtually all educational institutions had closed, as governments screamed their 'Stay at Home' messages in unison, across the world. Whilst the intention and the priority were both to control and contain the coronavirus, there were many unintended consequences that led to the revision of such directives and, in some cases, confusion.

Some of the emerging questions that politicians grappled with included: 1) What happens to 'vulnerable' children, including children with learning difficulties and those 'at risk', within the home environment? 2) What about children who depend on school meals for survival? 3) How would lessons be delivered, or instructions conducted, with learners who do not have access to internet and computers? 4) What would happen to exams, on which progression to the next level of education depended? 5) How could key workers or first responders continue to work, if their children were at home? 6) In the Global South, where teachers and instructors are the only resource for learners and school the only protection for the girl child, what happens? 7) For students nearing completion of courses and dissertations in Higher Education, what next? What about graduation? 8) What pressures could result in situations where a parent had several children of different age-groups confined in a small apartment, with one or no computer? 9) What about children whose parents did not have the capacity or resources to help them with their schoolwork? 10) Moreover, how would parents (many of whom were adjusting to working from home) supervise their children's schoolwork and do their own work, including virtual meetings? These are some of the questions to which there are no clear answers, and it will be years before some of the underlying issues can be addressed.

In the UK, students whose public exams were cancelled had their grades estimated by their teachers and submitted to the Exam Boards. The exam regulators, Ofqual (in England and Wales) and the Scottish Qualifications Authority (SQA), downgraded most of the teacher assessment grades, leading to mayhem, with knock-on effects on universities and college admissions and, undoubtedly, widespread stress among the candidates and their parents. Many Higher Education institutions reopened in late September and some quickly formed clusters of the coronavirus infection. Respective universities devised their own strategies, with most students staying in their accommodation and having food boxes left outside their doors.

RACE & RACE RELATED ISSUES

Race relations unmasked

2020 brought into sharp focus race and racialised issues that had been simmering, and in some cases been driven underground or dismissed, for many years. In America, twenty-two-year-old Japan-born tennis star Naomi Osaka wore black masks bearing different names, one for each game, of Black Americans who had been killed by the police. She went on to win the US Open, at New York's Flushing Meadows arena, watched by a handful of people, mainly those who worked at the arena.

National Football League (NFL) San Francisco 49ers quarterback, Colin Kaepernick, who had sat on a bench during the national anthem, on August 26th, 2016, as a protest against police brutality and racial injustice in the country soared to new heights. Later in 2016, his activism had become a talking point; undeterred, Kaepernick had changed to kneeling, rather than standing, during the anthem. His gesture, defended by former President Barack Obama as a constitutional right, enraged President Trump who described it as 'disrespecting the flag'. With ongoing polarisation at the highest political levels, Kaepernick had found himself an unsigned free agent, eventually out of the media spotlight. 2020 saw his protests receive new energised attention, following the death of George Floyd, a forty-six-year-old African American man, on May 26th in Minneapolis. A white policeman had been caught on camera kneeling on George Floyd's neck as Floyd protested, 'I can't breathe', until he stopped breathing.

Thanks to media coverage and social media sharing of video clips of the incident, protests began in Minneapolis and quickly spread to over 2,000 cities and towns and sixty countries across the World, under the banner of the 'Black Lives Matter (BLM)' movement. It is important to recognise the founders of BLM, before focusing on its current energy and momentum.

BLM was created by three Black females in America, in 2013, triggered by the acquittal of a security guard who had shot and killed a 17-year-old Black boy, Trayvon Martin, in Sanford, Florida. There were other unresolved killings of Black people by the police, like Breonna Taylor in Louisville and (more recently), Ahmaud Arbery in Georgia, that had angered the Black communities. The BLM founders were Patrisse Khan-Cullors from Los Angeles; Alicia Garza from Oakland (California); and New York-based Nigerian-American, Opal Tometi. All three women have become renowned activists, writers, strategists and are highly sought-after public speakers. BLM initially organised street protests highlighting the police killings of Black Americans, mainly Black men, and the associated injustice. BLM continued to engage with political and administrative structures, but it was the highly publicised killing of George Floyd that brought BLM to the world stage.

In Europe, BLM protests led to the toppling of statues that symbolised historical roots to racism and slavery. In the UK, the statues of Edward Colston (Bristol), Robert Milligan (London Docklands), Sir John Cass, Thomas Guy, and Robert Clayton (Central London). In USA the heightened race-related debates led to the removal of many Confederate personalities, including: Albert Pike (Washington DC), Charles Linn (Birmingham, AL), Christopher Columbus ('beheaded' in Boston, MA; St Paul, MN; Byrd Park, VA & Baltimore; Jefferson Davis & John Castleman, KY)). Elsewhere, more statues of personalities associated with mass ethnic killings fell or were vandalised, including: King Leopold II (Belgium-Congolese), John Hamilton (New Zealand-Maori) and Cecil Rhodes (South Africa). BLM activists and supporters saw these statues (and many others still under scrutiny) as a display 'celebrating' connections between contemporary racism to past historical roots. Critics (some staging counter-protests) focused on the damage caused by protesters' lawlessness and a claimed agenda to rewrite history.

Turning BLM Energy into Action

Celebrities, politicians, and sports stars used their platforms to add their voices to the BLM protests. English Premier League footballers habitually 'took the knee' before matches; while British Formula 1 driver Lewis Hamilton staged his own campaign, in support of BLM. To honour George Floyd, House Democrats 'took the knee' for 8 minutes and 46 seconds, the length of time the white policeman knelt on Floyd's neck, until he stopped breathing. Again, there were counter-protests, for example, shortly after kick-off of the Manchester City vs Burnley soccer game, on 24th June, a 'White Lives Matter' banner, in Burnley colours, was flown above the Etihad Stadium. On July 27th, NFL Black player, Stephon Tuitt refused to join his teammates kneeling during the national anthem, declaring that he is 'a proud American'. Meanwhile, the British Foreign Secretary, Dominic Raab, explained why he would not take the knee, which, in his view is a 'symbol of subjugation and subordination' and associated with the TV series Game of Thrones.

There have been many policy proposals that can be attributed to the BLM momentum, in 2020:

In America a bipartisan group, 20/20 Club, comprised of twenty Republican and twenty Democrat House Representatives, will hold forums at the two national party conventions, to press for change in Criminal Justice policies at Federal level. Broadly, public and private sectors are actively reviewing their narratives, employment, and remuneration policies, to avoid allegations and perceptions of racism. Whatever the future holds for California's Senator Kamala Harris, her nomination to become the running mate of the Democratic Party Presidential candidate, Joe Biden, on August 10th, is a historical moment. Born to immigrants of colour, a Jamaican father and Indian mother, Kamala Harris will be the first Black Woman to appear on a major party ticket. That is a big deal.

GLOBAL EVENTS THAT BECAME CASUALTIES

TOKYO

Global domino effect

On March 11th, the World Health Organisation declared the COVID-19 a pandemic and called on all countries to take urgent and aggressive action to protect health. Leaders would subsequently navigate the delicate balance between protecting lives on one hand and managing economic and social disruption on the other, with respect for human rights also in the mix. Based on the makeshift (often contradictory) daily briefings that followed, most leaders had been caught completely off-guard!

Once national and intergovernmental scientific teams highlighted the risk of spreading the novel coronavirus during public gatherings, a spotlight began to be shone on planned mega global and national events, including political, sports, religious, social, cultural and trade exhibitions. Given the time, financial and emotional resources invested in planning events like the Olympics, the real impact made by its postponement is beyond the scope of this project. Suffice to say it was painful to watch Japanese Prime Minister Shinzo Abe announce, on March 24th, the postponement of the Olympics to July 2021. Additional sports activities that fell victim were the Europewide soccer tournament, Euro 2020, which retained the 2020 name but was postponed to 2021; the London, New York and Boston marathons; international tennis tournaments, including Wimbledon, Paris Open, and US Open, were cancelled or rescheduled. The Six Nations rugby tournament, which was drawing to a close, was postponed to October.

Political, Cultural and Religious Events

Rather than cancelling major sports activities altogether, some organising bodies decided to reopen and proceed without spectators. It must have been odd for major soccer league players to score goals and win trophies and not be able to celebrate with their fans in the stands. After thirty years, Liverpool FC were presented with the coveted English Premier League trophy, without the adoring Anfield crowd. Arsenal FC won the FA cup, Real Madrid clinched the La Liga title, while Bayern Munich and Juventus were crowned winners of the Bundesliga and Serie A competitions, respectively. All the presentations took place in eerily empty stadia! Similarly, the final matches of the money-spinning European elite soccer competition, the UEFA Champions League, were played in an empty stadium in Portugal. The Diamond League athletics competition that had been rescheduled to August saw Uganda's Joshua Cheptegei break his own 5km world record, cheered on by a small socially-distanced 'crowd'. Cheptegei set another world record when he won the 10Km race in Valencia, on October 7th.

The rescheduled London marathon was reduced to only elite runners and run in laps around St James Park, rather than the usual scenic route around different London landmarks; the winners were Ethiopia's Shura Kitata (men) and Kenya's Brigid Kosgei (women). The unusual conditions opened opportunities for wider participation which saw a total of 45,000 people from 109 countries complete the 26.2-mile race in their home areas.

The French Open, also rescheduled to October was won by Polish teenager, Iga Swiatek, who clinched the Women's trophy and veteran Rafael Nadal who won the Men's to equal Roger Federer's record of 20 Grand Slam titles.

Organisers of other events and conventions had reluctantly began contemplating the unthinkable; could they, would they reschedule or cancel monumental events like Dubai's Expo 2020? After weeks of speculation, the uncomfortable answer that came out repeatedly was 'yes'! Like dominos, global events continued to capitulate to the invisible menace – the novel coronavirus.

Intergovernmental organisation summits that had been scheduled to discuss global issues were also postponed, in some cases, new dates and formats – scaled down or virtual – have yet to be named. They include the annual G7 (Group of 7) summit; the G7 is comprised of the world's seven richest countries – Canada, France, Germany, Italy, Japan, the United Kingdom, and United States of America. Each member nation takes over the G7 presidency for a year on a rotational basis and 2020 was the turn of the USA. The Summit was initially expected to take place at Camp David, in June; it was postponed to September and discussions about a new date are underway.

The 26th United Nations Climate Change Conference (UNFCCC COP26), scheduled for November 2020 in Glasgow, UK, was postponed to November 2021. COP26 stands for Conference of the Parties and it brings together 184 countries that have signed the UN Framework Convention on Climate Change (UNFCCC), a treaty that entered into force in March 1994.

Annual religious events that attract global participation fell, starting with one of the most important events in the Christian calendar – Easter. The climax celebration for this would have been a service presided over by the Pope on the balcony of a (usually) packed St Peter's Square, at the Vatican. Easter church services were cancelled across the world and the 1.3 billion Roman Catholics settled for a virtual blessing.

Next was the Muslim festival of Hajj, which normally draws together about 2.5 million world-wide pilgrims to the holy cities of Mecca and Madina to partake in the week-long once-in-a-lifetime duty for every able-bodied Muslim who can afford it. For the first time in the history of Saudi Arabia, the government banned all but 1,000 or so participants who were already residing in the country.

Annual cultural and music festivals, to which regular participants attach emotional significance, were also axed due to COVID-19. They included St Patrick's Day parades across the world (March 17th), Britain's Edinburgh Festival and Glastonbury, which had been expected to welcome the legendary Paul McCartney and America's Taylor Swift. Also cancelled were the Eurovision Contest, which had been due to take place in Rotterdam.

WEATHER AND OTHER NATURAL PHENOMENA

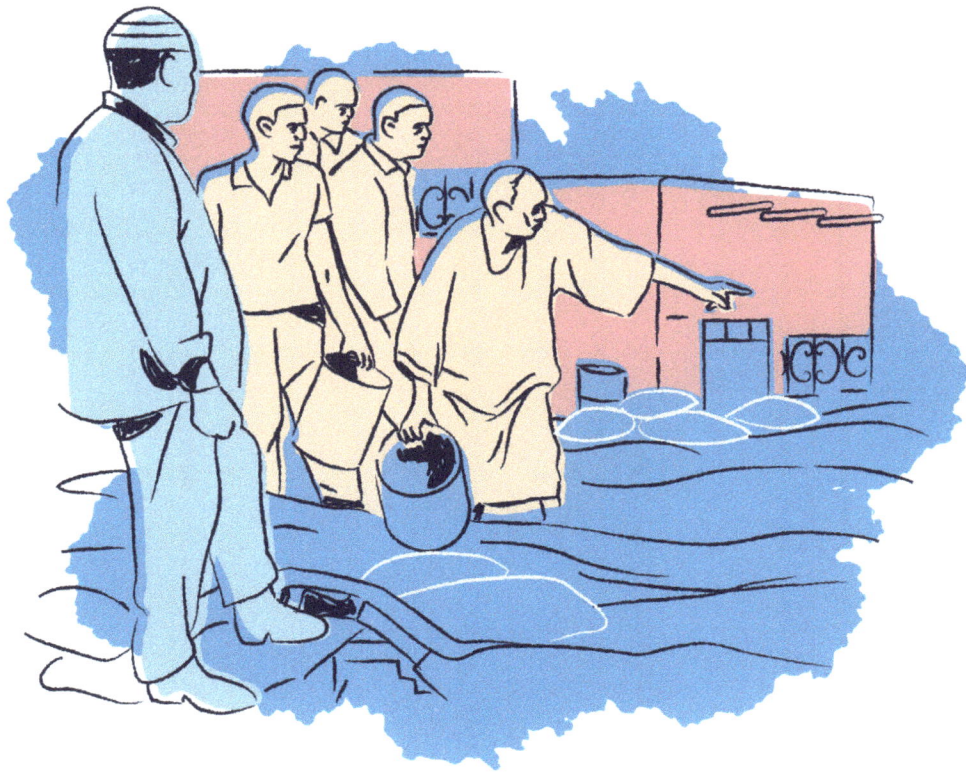

Europe, Asia, the Caribbean region, and the Gulf of Mexico had their warmest January–July since regional records began in 1910.

Record-warm July temperatures were widespread across the North Indian Ocean, south-eastern Asia, and the western Pacific Ocean. Other areas with record-warm July temperatures were present across parts of the Caribbean Sea, northern South America, North America, and the North Pacific Ocean.

According to the European Union's observation programme, Copernicus, (i) September 2020 was the warmest on record, globally; (ii) the Arctic sea ice is at its second lowest since satellite records began.

To mitigate the doom and gloom outlook to environmental issues Britain's Prince William and renowned Sir David Attenborough on October 8th jointly launched the Earthshot Prize, described as the 'Nobel Prize for Environmentalism'. With a $65 million fund five recipients of the annual award will receive $1.3 million each, for innovations that provide solutions to the world's environmental challenges.

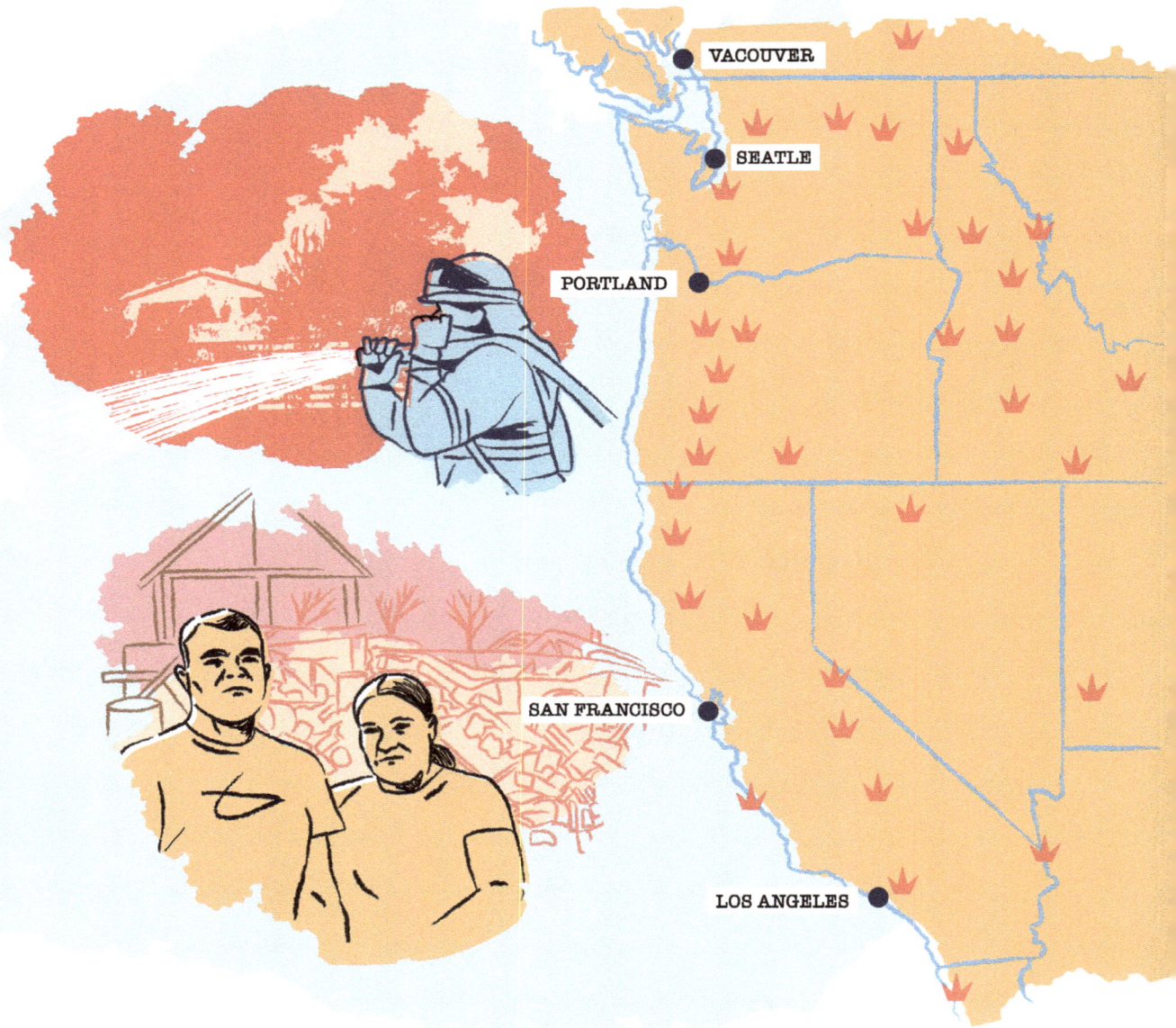

USA fires

On September 9th the sky turned orange over California and Oregon.

According to California State Fire Department, CAL FIRE, five of the top 20 largest wildfires in California history have occurred in 2020. Since the beginning of the year, there have been over 8,100 wildfires that have burned over 3.7 million acres in California. On September 15th, a BBC report contextualised the raging fires as the equivalent of 1000 football fields burning every 30 minutes.

While debate rages between scientists and politicians, regarding the underlying causes of fire; climate change vs forest management, the fires that have ravaged California and Arizona have inflicted far-reaching consequences. A report in 2015, for the US Department of Agriculture suggested another indirect cause as being the increase in internal migration, from urban to forest areas, thereby increasing vulnerability of the new dwellers. Altogether, lives and livelihoods have been lost and impact on air quality has been felt thousands of miles away, in New York and Washington DC. The Sydney Morning Herald of September 16th reported plumes in the Jetstream carried across the to the Northeast coast of the USA through to mid-Atlantic. CAL FIRE estimates that, between August 15th and September 27th there had been over 26 fatalities and over 7,000 structures had been destroyed. CAL FIRE attributes 2020 fires to 'unusually strong winds combined with periods of drought across western parts of USA.

USA hurricanes

When Tropical Storm Beta landed on the shores of Texas, USA, on September 22nd it was the ninth named landfall storm in 2020, equalling the previous record set in 1916. Given previous occurrences of at least one tropical storm in October and November, it is likely that 2020 will set a record for the highest number of tropical storms in a single year.

The leading explanation reported by The Washington Post (September 24) is the record sea surface temperature (SST) in the Tropical Atlantic, including the Gulf of Mexico, which creates rapid evaporation and subsequent heavy downpours.

By missing the heavily populated areas of New Orleans and Houston the damage caused by the numerous hurricanes has been less severe than previous ones such as Katrina and Rita.

Floods

On July 9th devastating floods swept across large parts of China and Japan. Every summer southern parts of China are affected by heavy rains leading to widespread flooding. This year's floods began in early June and were exceptionally violent due to El Nino impact and increase in vapour from the Pacific Ocean and Indian Ocean. By early July China's Ministry of Water Resources reported that 33 of the 433 rivers had recorded the highest ever flood levels. The ravaging floods had claimed over 140 victims and displaced over 38 million people in the most affected regions of Guizhou, Guangxi, Sichuan, Hubei, Chongqing, Anhui, Jiangxi, Zhejiang, Hunan, Fujian, and Yunnan.

In early October Storm Alex swept across Europe and caused downpours of half a meter in a day, on two occasions. The resulting deadly flash floods in Southern France and Northern Italy destroyed property and killed at least 7 people.

In the same period Japan Meteorological Agency reported rainfall rates of 98mm per hour in Hioki City in Kagoshima, on July 6th . Over 20 fatalities were confirmed, with a further 20 reported as missing.

Deadly floods swept across many African countries too. In 11 West and Central African countries around 760,000 people were affected, with 110 killed. Between July and September over 330,000 people had been affected in Niger, especially in the capital city, Niamey, where a dam on River Niger collapsed. In neighbouring Burkina Faso, a state of emergency was declared, following destruction of thousands of homes, roads, and bridges. A further 103 were reported dead and over 166,000 houses destroyed in Sudan.

In Ethiopia where rains surpassed previous records set in 1946 and 1988 a three-month state of emergency was declared, to mobilise support for over 144,000 people displaced by the Awash River.

In Uganda's capital city, Kampala, two bodies were recovered following flash floods, on September 11th. On September 13th floods triggered the collapse of a mine in the Democratic Republic of Congo, leaving 50 dead.

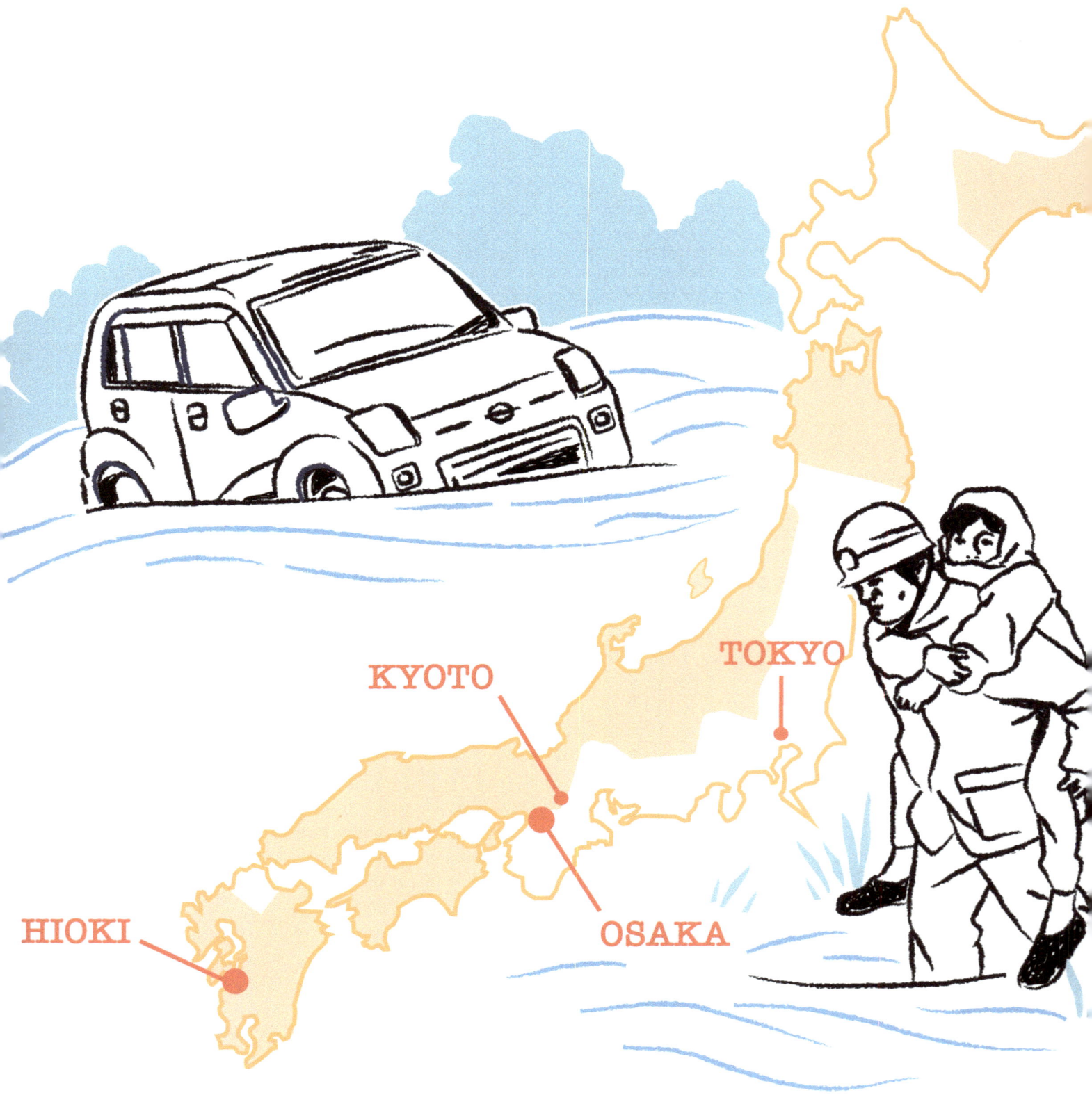

KYOTO

TOKYO

OSAKA

HIOKI

Whales beached in Tasmania

Perhaps one of the most upsetting reports and images (illustrations withheld) etched in our minds in 2020 is that of 380 whales that have died in what is suspected to be Australia's largest stranding on record. Reasons for the tragic occurrence remain unclear. Scientists have suggested a range of theories, including disorientation due to failure to detect a relatively shallow coastline, by the 'community' of whales that normally travel together. Credit to the hardworking dedicated team of 60 rescuers who managed to escort at least 50 whales back into the sea.

GOVERNMENTS FIND MONEY TREES

'Billion' & 'Trillion' become everyday words

The threat of businesses collapsing due to lockdown, and the potential for mass unemployment, prompted governments and central banks to make some unprecedented financial decisions to mitigate potentially disastrous outcomes.

In March, the Australian government unveiled a $189 billion coronavirus economic rescue package, including an extra $550 a fortnight for the unemployed. The Chinese government implemented a combination of fiscal (tax-related), monetary, financial and trade policies to keep the economy running. After prolonged negotiations, the European Union agreed a 'coronavirus recovery deal' in July of 1.82 trillion euros, to help mitigate the economic consequences of the coronavirus in member countries. Individual European Governments had already implemented some emergency rescue packages in their respective countries.

Japan released a Cabinet Decision entitled 'Emergency Economic Measures To Cope With COVID-19' in April, of about $1 trillion to help businesses survive.

In the UK, after unveiling a wartime budget of £330 billion in March, the UK Chancellor of Exchequer, Rishi Sunak, repeatedly promised to 'do whatever it takes' to help British people and British businesses, with an additional £27.4 billion for furloughed employees and about £43 billion in loans for businesses; including the famous 'Eat out to help out' government offer to split the food bill with customers (capped at £10) eating at restaurants on Monday to Wednesday, during the month of August. In April, the USA approved a $6 trillion stimulus package; and discussions for the next stimulus package are underway between Congress and the White House team.

DEBATE 2020

ELECTIONS OF THE 46th USA PRESIDENT

A break from norms

From virtual National Party Conventions, to abrasive presidential debates through to questioning of electoral processes and votes, the US elections provided a spectacle to add the uniqueness of 2020.

National Party Conventions where presumptive nominees formally become presidential candidates are usually large colourful events in the USA's election calendar. The current pandemic caused major disruptions to planned events, that were recalibrated in accordance with State regulations. The four-day Democratic event originally planned to take place in Milwaukee, Wisconsin took place from remote locations, with Joe Biden delivering his acceptance speech over a live video stream from his home in Delaware.

The Republican National Convention took place with limited in-person participation, in Charlotte, North Carolina. Unlike previous RNCs where participants adopt a 'platform'/manifesto the Republicans passed a one-page resolution stating that the party 'has and will continue to enthusiastically support the president's America-first agenda'.

Drive-in Democratic vs

crowded Republican rallies

Democratic Candidate Biden and his surrogates opted for socially distanced drive-in campaigns, usually in car parks. During these rallies, attendees parked their cars around the stage, often in front of a large projector screen to help visibility. In addition to social distancing most of the audience were seen wearing masks for extra protection against COVID-19.

President Trump's rallies, on the other hand, were attended by thousands of supporters, who neither social distanced nor wore masks; for example, in Nevada, where the crowd exceeded the state's restriction on gatherings to 50.

While President Trump mocked thinly attended 'Sleepy Joe' Biden's rallies through his Twitter messages, telling his supporters in Florida that he wanted to 'kiss everyone in the audience..', Joe Biden declared Trump's rallies 'criminal' for putting lives at risk of contracting COVID-19. It is worth remembering that attendees at a rally in Oklahoma were reportedly asked to sign a waiver absolving the president's campaign of any liability from virus related illnesses.

Presidential debates (or rants)?

Words such as 'mess', 'off-putting', 'embarrassing', 'disgusting', 'car-crash' were used to describe the first of three presidential debates held between the two presidential candidates, Trump and Biden, on 29th September. The level of indiscipline displayed during the first debate, moderated by veteran journalist Chris Wallace led the Commission on Presidential Debates to consider muting microphones in subsequent debates.

The second debate scheduled for 9th October was cancelled due to the President's COVID-19 diagnosis. Instead each candidate took part in a separate town-hall (question-and-answer) event, aired simultane-ously. The final debate which took place on October 22nd was a more civil one, with credit given to the NBC moderator, Kristen Welker.

The Vice-Presidential debate on October 7th took on a new significance, demonstrated by the high number of viewers (approximately 58 million compared to 36 million in 2016). Some observers attributed the interest to the possibility of Kamala Harris taking on presidential duties, in case of a Democratic win.

President and First Lady contract COVID-19

On the morning of October 2nd, the world read a stunning tweet from President Trump,

'Tonight @FLOTUS and I tested positive for COVID-19. We will begin our quarantine and recovery process immediately. We will get through this TOGETHER!'

The announcement was followed by tumultuous events that included the President being airlifted to the Walter Reed National Medical Center for treatment, uncoordinated updates by the medical team, several White House staffers testing positive to COVID-19 and cancellation of scheduled events. The President posted a video of himself, with a reassuring message to his supporters. The president attributed his fast recovery, return to work and rallies to the cocktail of new therapies he had taken. The First Lady, on the other hand took the option of taking time out for recovery.

Pollsters proved wrong – again!

Opinion pollsters were, once again, spectacularly wrong. Four years after Hillary Clinton who had been widely expected to win lost the election to Donald Trump. Pollsters claimed to have learnt lessons from the mistakes of 2016, yet in 2020 poll after poll held just before the election day gave Democratic Candi-date Joe Biden a 10-12% margin lead nationally and smaller margins in 'swing' states. The result was much narrower. In the House of Representatives Democrats had been expected to increase their majority; al-though they held on to the control of the House, they suffered a net loss of 6 seats. In the Senate polls had indicated that Democrats had a chance of flipping marginal seats such as Maine, with a chance of taking control of the Senate. As results came in on election night, starting with the Presidential win in Florida, through to Senator Susan Collins retaining Maine, it became apparent that the predicted landslide win for Democrats was not going to happen. The pollsters had got it wrong. Again.

The Biden-Harris duo:

Jill's husband and the first female, first

black vice president-elect.

2020 US elections were even more extraordinary when they ended with both candidates claiming victory. By numbers, 270 electoral votes are required for a win. Joe Biden appeared to have 306 (290 con-firmed) electoral votes, the incumbent, Republican had 232; the popular vote (as it stands) is 78,114,089 to 72,741,954 in favour of Joe Biden so it was intrigu-ing to hear the Secretary of State, Mike Pompeo, talking about transition to the second Trump term. There remain countless lawsuits and vote recounts in place so the final outcome will not be known until January 2021, after the Georgia runoff. There is no law that requires the loser in the Presidential election to concede, it is simply a tradition that began in 1896 by Democrat William Jennings Bryan, after losing to Republican William McKinley. But Donald Trump is a president who has his own set of norms, so the drama continues as the world watches uncomfortably and waits for January 20th, 2021.

Meanwhile, On 11th August 2020 presumptive Democratic Party Presidential (then) candidate Joe Biden ended speculation of which woman he would choose as a running mate, by audaciously naming California's Senator, Kamala Harris, who had recently been his opponent in the race for nomination. Regardless of ideological views and political affiliations the nomination was historical. Kamala Harris, a daughter of immigrants (Professor Donald Harris from Jamaica and Shyamala Gopalan, a scientist and activist from India) who had been the first Asian-American woman in the US Senate became the first woman of colour to appear on a national election ballot paper in the USA. The decision taken by the (now president-elect) Joe Biden who introduced himself as 'Jill's husband' and introduced Kamala and her husband Douglas, as part of the 'Biden family' is monumental. With multiple identities Kamala Harris will be the first female, first Africa-American, first Asian-American and first Caribbean-American vice president. A Vice President of the USA has to be ready to govern, should anything happen to- or render the President incapable of governing; Joe Biden knew (and knows) this. It is this thought that causes jitters and unease among some, for example Britain's Lord Kilclooney who Twitted "What happens if Biden moves on and the Indian becomes President. Who then becomes Vice President?"

What does Kamala Harris say?

She and Joe are ready to govern. Some of the most memorable lines from her victory speech include recognition of the black women before her on whose shoulders she stands. She paid tribute to her mother, Shyamala who raised her and her sister Maya, as a single parent. Addressing the little girls watching her, she declared that she '…might be the first in this position but I won't be the last'. Kamala Harris's shattering of the political glass ceiling in the USA brings hope to many women, especially overlooked women of colour. Not far behind Harris is a pool of rising black women, for example Stacey Abrams whose efforts in addressing voter suppres-sion inspired change in the previously Repub-lican state of Georgia and Atlanta's Mayor, Keisha Lance Bottoms who was thrust into the limelight, at the peak of the Black Lives Matter demonstra-tions. Worthy of recognition for the success of the Biden-Harris campaign is another formidable woman, the campaign manager, Jen O'Malley Dillon described by many outlets simply as 'a master'. Who can argue?

ACTS OF KINDNESS AND INSPIRATION

Captain Sir Tom Moore

Captain Sir Tom Moore needs no introduction after he raised in excess of £32m for UK's National Health Service, as he celebrated his 100th birthday. The occasion was also marked with Royal Air Force flypast and birthday greetings from HM Queen Elizabeth II and British PM Boris Johnson. Above all, he inspired many to follow in his footsteps and consider their own acts of kindness and fundraising; some are featured here.

Dame Vera Lynn

Dame Vera Lynn was best known for performing hits such as We'll Meet Again to WW2 troops on the frontlines overseas, including in India and Egypt. Ahead of the 75th anniversary of Victory in Europe (VE) Day, and during the height of the coronavirus pandemic, Dame Vera beat her own record when she became the oldest artist to get a top 40 album in the UK, after her greatest hits album re-entered the charts at number 30. HM The Queen echoed her famous WW2 anthem during a speech to Britons separated from families and friends during the coronavirus lockdown in April, telling the nation: "We will be with our friends again, we will be with our families again, and we will meet again." Dame Vera Lynn passed away on 18th June, at her home in East Sussex. A commemoration coin was released by the London Mint to raise funds for the Dame Vera Lynn Charitable Trust.

Joan Willet

Joan Willet, a former teacher who lives at Old Hastings House residential home in East Sussex in UK, marked her 104th birthday by completing an epic fundraising challenge, which has raised more than £35,000 for British Heart Foundation. Inspired by Sir Tom Moore, Willet used her daily exercise regime of walking up and down a steep hill to raise the funds for research, which she says helped her get past her 100th birthday.

Alfons Leempoels

Alfons Leempoels a 103-year-old retired Belgian Doctor, also inspired by Captain Tom Moore, walked a marathon to raise funds for research, for the nearby University of Leuven, where researchers are working to find a cure for COVID-19. He walked ten laps of 145 metres (159 yards); three in the morning, three at noon and four in the evening. To avoid losing count, he threw a stick into a bowl every time he completed a lap. Later, Leempoels said of his achievement.

"My children said that I can walk at least as well as Tom Moore and on top of that I am 103 years old," he told Reuters.

Marcus Rashford

Marcus Rashford is a Manchester United and England soccer star. In an open emotional letter to the British Government, the twenty-two-year-old made a compelling plea to address child poverty. He cited his own childhood experience as one of five children raised by a single mother and a beneficiary of food vouchers. Rashford's letter led to the extension of a government policy to provide free school meals for children, which was due to end with the school term. Rashford had, earlier during lockdown, teamed up with a food charity, FareShare, an initiative that raised over £20 million to provide school meals. The project was initially set up to provide meals in the Greater Manchester area, but it expanded into a national initiative.

Sette Buenaventura

Sette Buenaventura, a British twenty-six-year-old nurse from Eccles, ignored intense pain in her right calf, due to work commitments at the Salford Royal Hospital in Manchester. She later had her leg amputated, due to a sarcoma (a malignant tumour). Explaining why she put off her own medical issues, Buenaventura said, "When Covid-19 kicked off, we worked flat out, we didn't have time to worry about aches and pains."

Annmarie Plas

Annmarie Plas, a thirty-six-year-old Dutch national living in London, UK, with her British husband and child, spontaneously created the 'Clap-for-Carers' movement to show support for frontline workers battling COVID-19. The movement quickly became a weekly phenomenon and British households (including PM Boris Johnson and British Royals) came out to clap, every Thursday, at 8pm.

Patrick Hutchinson

Patrick Hutchinson, a BLM protester, in a selfless act carried an injured white man who was counter-protesting with the British Far Right movement. Hutshinson, a personal trainer from South London, told a CNN reporter that he had 'no idea who this man was... (he) wasn't there to support BLM... (he) was just trying to avoid a catastrophe'. The white anti-BLM protester turned out to be a former policeman. British PM, Boris Johnson was reported to have been moved by Hutchinson's bravery.

Aaron Plummer

Aaron Plummer, a 19-year-old resident of Walthamstow completed his 26.2-mile London Marathon, in aid of Mencap, a UK charity that supports people with learning disabilities. Undeterred by his own learning disabilities and cerebral palsy, Aaron was spurred on by the support he and others have received from Mencap. Like other non-elite participants Aaron completed his virtual race in his home area of Walthamstow and raised over £30,000 for what he described as '....the greatest charity ever.'

Cody Krabbendam

Cody Krabbendam, a seven-year-old boy from British Columbia, Canada, received an award for bravery, for jumping into Shuswap Lake at Sicamous's beach park on July 11th to save another boy from drowning. According to his mother, Kim Krabbendam, Cody 'didn't think… he just jumped in because that's what people do.'

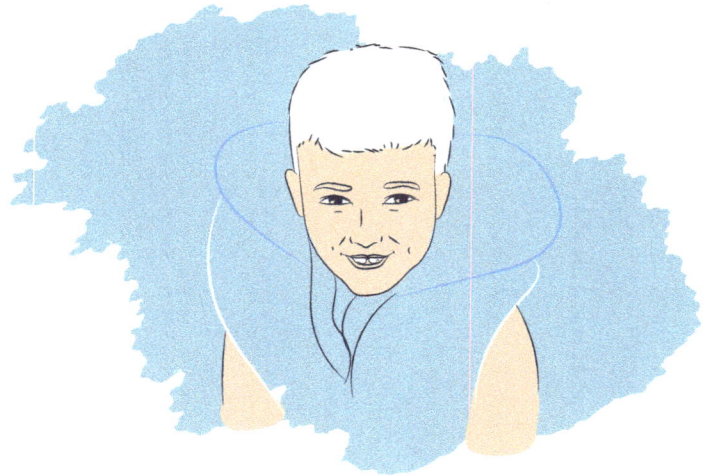

Haitham and Mumin Aamer

Haitham and Mumin Aamer are two Iraqi brothers who own the Grand House restaurant in Mosul. They supplied free meals to al-Batool hospital medical and health staff during night shifts so that monitoring of coronavirus cases could continue 24/7.

Alvaro Ramon

Alvaro Ramon, a cattle farmer and milk supplier in the Amazon region of Ecuador, decided to drive his truck and distribute milk freely to at least twenty home-steads in his Huamboya community during lockdown.

YOUNG ENTREPRENEURS EMERGING DURING LOCKDOWN

In June, the UK-based AdamStart, founded by Adam Bradford (reported to be stranded in Benin, West Africa, due to lockdown), announced the four winners of the 2020 competition. This year competitors were set the task of tackling coronavirus in their communities. The winners were:

Juliet Namujju, 23, from Mpigi, Uganda who designed a cotton African-print face mask that is reusable and biodegradable, which is also adapted to allow lip-reading. At least 2,000 masks have been distributed, free of charge, to market vendors and passenger motor-bicycles ('boda boda') riders in Kampala. Namujju, who was orphaned at seven years of age, was raised by her single grandmother and was surrounded by disability that inspired her mask design.

Patrick Sseremba, 23, from Kampala, Uganda, adapted his mobile medical innovation to deliver digital on-demand medical and dental services to rural communities during the lockdown.

Apoorv Shankar, 29, from Bangalore, India devised a hand-key, a sliding hand-held clamp that helped to open and push ATM buttons and manipulate other potentially contaminated public surfaces.

Osama Bin Noor, 29, from Dhakar, Bangladesh, designed a programme to connect young people and their ideas to policymakers, ensuring that communities in rural Bangladesh got support during the pandemic.

Dmytril Lavrinenko, 27, from Kiev, Ukraine created an online skills-sharing platform to help those who were disconnected.

Nicholas Bubeck, a six-year-old from Arizona, USA, became the youngest business owner and CEO of Creations by Nicholas. Nicholas created paper planes for himself and his young brother, initially to keep busy during lockdown, but he developed the idea into a business that currently sells build-your-own paper-plane kits, to instil in children creativity, imagination and love for travel.

NATIONAL LEADERS CATAPULTED TO THE WORLD STAGE

2020 will, undoubtedly, be remembered for the direct toll on human lives and livelihoods, and indirect toll on human activity. The World Health Organisation regularly provided general information and guidelines and it was up to national leaders to adapt the broad guidelines to their domestic situations, so they could protect the health and lives of their citizens. Here, we see examples of national leaders, judged favourably by multiple sources:

Jacinta Ardern

Under the leadership of Prime Minister Jacinda Arden, 40, New Zealand is referenced by Kevin Kunzman in Contagion Live, Aug 9th, as 'emblematic champion of proper prevention and response to the coronavirus 2019 (COVID-19) pandemic'. New Zealand, an island of five million people, diagnosed the first COVID-19 victim on February 26th, around the same time as concerns reverberated across the world about the severe symptoms of the SARS-CoV-2. By the end of the month, an influenza pandemic plan was in action, including border controls, culminating in lockdown on March 24th. There was a dramatic switch in strategy, from mitigating to eliminating the disease. At the time of writing, New Zealand had registered fewer than 1,600 cases, 22 deaths and is marking 100 days without 'community spread'.

Jacinta Arden, quoted by BBC as having gone 'hard and early' (Anna Jones, July 10th), says she 'did a little dance' the day New Zealand was declared COVID-19 free, in June.

Unsurprisingly, Jacinta Ardern was re-elected for a second term as Prime Minister in October, with a resounding majority in an election where her handling of C-19 was thought to be a decisive factor.

Tsai Ing-wen

Taiwan and Iceland have also been praised for the cooperative strategies they adopted in response to the COVID-19 pandemic.

Under the leadership of President (and academic) Tsai Ing-wen, 64, Taiwan, an island with a population of 23.8 million people had, by June 30th, recorded only 474 cases and 7 deaths, with 435 fully recovered. CNBC reporters Christina Farr and Michelle Gao (July 15th) outline Taiwan's effective measures, which included 1) Travel ban and quarantine, 2) A clear plan [adapted from the SARS 2003 model for managing pandemics] and no exceptions, 3) Getting ahead of mask shortages, 4) Regular communication with the public, 5) The digital health care system, and 6) Community mindedness, a willingness for people to sacrifice individual pleasures for the sake of their community.

Katrin Jackobsdottir

With regards to Iceland, Elizabeth Kolbert's report in the New Yorker (June 1st) is introduced with a powerful statement: 'The country didn't just manage to flatten the curve; it virtually eliminated it.' The first known case of COVID-19 in Iceland was recorded on February 28th.. Immediately, the team that had just been instituted traced all fifty-six people who had been within six feet of the victim and ordered them to quarantine themselves for fourteen days. Despite this quick response, by mid-March there was an onslaught from the virus. However, Iceland did not impose a lockdown, focusing instead on testing and sequencing to identify where the person who tested positive had been and imposing the two-meter social distancing rule. It is rumoured that all of Iceland's 365,000 people are related (check out PM Katrin's family contacts), which may have aided tracing and tracking, but credit must be accorded to Prime Minister, Katrin Jackobsdottir's coalition government for keeping coronavirus cases under 2,000 with only ten deaths.

What do the leaders above have in common? Former IMF chief, Christine Lagarde describes the work done by these leaders as 'stunning' and is quoted in The Independent (UK, July 24th) as 'I would say that for myself I've learnt that women tend to do a better job.' She added, 'This is my woman's bias and I indulge in ceding to this bias.' What appears to play out from these few examples is the successful navigation of protecting life versus economic outcomes; looking at the long-term, versus immediate gratification; you may have your own views!

There are other countries that deserve commendation, as of August 15th, for keeping reported COVID-19 deaths between zero and ten, namely, Uganda, Vietnam, Mongolia, Eritrea, Namibia, Gibraltar, Cambodia, Bhutan, Seychelles, French Polynesia, Macao, Lesotho and Papua New Guinea.

E-COMMERCE: THE BIG WINNERS

Demise of brick and motar?

When human activity, especially movement stopped, to contain the coronavirus, the alternative way to work (except key workers/emergency services), shop, get entertainment and communicate was via the internet. The big winners during the lockdown were the established players in the digital space and those that quickly found entry points.

Three names are appended to an unfamiliar word, 'centibillionaires', to define a net worth of $100 billion or over. They are American: Bill Gates, founder of Microsoft; Jeff Bezos, founder of Amazon; and Mark Zuckerberg, founder of Facebook. Mid-way into 2020 they have added an estimated $44 billion, $75 billion, and $22 billion, respectively, to their net worth. Some sources add Frenchman Bernard Arnault, 70, who controls the luxury portfolio that includes Louis Vuitton, Hennessy Cognac, Dom Perignon Champagne, Tag Heuer watches, and Christian Dior fashion range as having joined the club of centibillionaires in August.

Previously less well-known Zoom Communications Inc., based in San Jose, California, quickly became a household phenomenon and a commonly accepted verb. Meetings, social conversations, parties, church services, funerals and lessons were soon being held via Zoom. Other platforms emerged, including Microsoft Teams, and upgraded Skype, and many others. All of these benefitted from increased revenue from subscriptions.

Other digital businesses that appear to have cannibalised the traditional brick-and-mortar traders include the Dubai-based Jumia, dubbed the 'Amazon of Africa', the largest e-commerce company on the continent, which has spiked four-fold after having run into difficulties in 2019. Also, Abidjan-based Afrikea, an e-commerce platform for African fashion designers, mainly serving Europe and USA, realised a three-fold increase in orders. However, both platforms experienced difficulties due to interruptions in supplies sourced from China.

Finally, the world of fitness and entertainment saw spikes in demand for online fitness classes, while bicycle sales also soared. With cinemas and theatres indefinitely shut, demand for the American-based Netflix services exploded, so did YouTube searches for music and other entertainment.

IN MEMORIAM

We think of each family whose life has been changed by the loss of a loved one in 2020.
Here we name some of them and illustrate a few..

Diego Maradona (Soccer star)

Dave Prowse (Actor and bodybuilder)

Ray Clemence (Soccer star - goalkeeper)

Des O'Connor (Presenter and entertainer)

Spinbad - Chris Sullivan (Musician)

Melvin Noble - M03 (Musician)

Bert Belasco (Actor)

Bones Hillman (Musician)

John Fraser (Actor)

King Von (Musician)

Geoffrey Palmer (Actor)

Joy Westmore (Actor)

Ken Hensley (Musician)

Elsa Raven (Actor)

Lawrence Clayton (Actor)

John Sessions (Performer)

Carol Arthur (Actor)

Eddie Hassell (Actor)

Nikki McKibbin (TV star)

Sir Sean Connery (Actor)

Julie Donaldson (Persenter & Activist

Luis Troyano (TV star)

Nate Burrell (Docuseries star)

Marius Zaliukas (Soccer star)

Nobby Stiles (Soccer star)

JJ Williams (Rugby star)

Bobby Ball (Performer)

Billy Joe Shaver (Musician)

Tony Wyn-Jones (Broadcaster)

Johnny Leeze (Actor)

Frank Bough (TV Presenter)

Marge Champion (Dancer and Broadway star)

James Randi (Magician and scientific skeptic)

Spencer Davis (Founder of the Spencer Davis Group)

Tony Lewis (Singer in The Outfield)

José Padilla (DJ)

Dana Baratta (Writer and producer)

Doreen Montalvo (Broadway star)

Anthony Chisholm (Actor)

Gordon Haskell (Musician)

Tony Lewis (Singer in The Outfield)

Rhonda Fleming (Actor)

Paul Matters (Musician)

Saint Dog (Singer in The Outfield)

Conchata Ferrell (Actor)

Carmen Sevilla (Actor & singer)

Bunny Lee (Musician)

Johnny Nash (Musician)

Eddie Van Halen (Musician)

Margaret Nolan (Actor)

Clark Middleton (Actor, Director and producer)

Kenzo Takada (Founder and designer of Kenzo products)

Thomas Jefferson Byrd (Actor)

DJ Cookie Monsta (DJ)

Frank Windsor (Actor)

Helen Reddy (Musician)

Dean Jones (Cricketer)

Juliette Greco (Musician)

Archie Lyndhurst (Actor)

Michael Lonsdale (Actor, director and author)

Jackie Stallone (Astrolger and publicist)

Tommy DeVito (Fonding member of The Four Seasons)

IN MEMORIAM

EJ Osborne (Presenter)

Lee Kerslake (Musician)

Pamela Hutchinson (Musician)

Alien Huang (Performer and designer)

Pat Smullen (Jockey)

Sei Ashina (Actor)

Sir Terence Conran (Founder of Habitat)

Toots Hibbert (Musician)

Dame Diana Rigg (Actor)

Ronald Bell (Founding member Kool & the Gang)

Stevie Lee (Actor and wrestler)

Alan Minter (Boxer)

Simeon Coxe (Musician)

Aaron Grissom (Reality TV start and chef)

Anna Norbury (Actor)

Kevin Dobson (Actor)

Bruce Williamson (Musician)

Rodney Litchfield (Actor)

Annie Cordy (Performer)

Ian Mitchell (Musician)

Ian Royce (Reality TV star)

Cloyd Robinson (Actor)

Steve Lee (Sports journalist)

Riley Gale (Musician)

Allan Rich (Actor)

Landon Clifford (Social media star)

Jack Sherman (Musician)

Chi Chi DeVayne (TV star)

Trini Lopez (Musician and actor)

Wayne Fontana (Musician)

FGB Duck (Musician)

Brian Black (Presenter)

Brent Carver (Actor)

John Hume (Politician)

Wilford Brimley (Actor)

Reni Santoni (Actor)

Tony Morris (TV presenter)

Denise Johnson (Musician)

Peter Green (Co-founder Fleetwood Mac)

Jack Charlton (Soccer star)

Louis Mahoney (Actor)

Carl Reiner (Actor)

Joel Schumacher (Producer)

Ian Holm (Actor)

Willie Thorne (Snooker legend)

Michael Angelis (Actor)

Tony Scannel (Actor)

Mory Kante (Musician)

Fred Willard (Actor)

Little Richard (Musician)

Ben Chijioke (Musician)

Brian Howe (Musician)

Florian Schneider (Musician)

June Bernicoff (TV star)

Sam Lloyd (Actor)

Tony Allen (Musician)

Irrfan Khan (Actor)

BJ Hogg (Actor)

Jill Gascoine (Actor)

Lynn Faulds Wood (Presenter and journalist)

Neil Black (Athlete)

Ebow Graham (Musician)

IN MEMORIAM

Norman Hunter (Soccer star)

Howard Finkel (Sports presenter)

Ranjit Chowdhry (Actor)

Brian Dennehy (Actor)

Sean Arnold (Actor)

Tim Brooke-Taylor (Actor)

Sir Stirling Moss (Motor-racing legend)

Black The Ripper (Dean West) (Artist)

James Drury (Actor)

Honor Blackman (Actor)

Vinolia Mashego (TV star)

James King (Reality TV star)

Bill Withers (Musician)

Eddie Large (Performer)

Logan Williams (Actor)

Joe Diffie (Musician)

John Callahan (Actor)

Mark Blum (Actor)

Kenny Rogers (Musician)

Lorenzo Brino (Actor)

Max von Sydow (Actor)

Dave Rainford (Presenter)

Danny Tidwell (Performer)

Nicholas Tucci (Actor)

Michael Medwin (Actor)

Simon Warr (Broadcaster)

Boris Leskin (Actor)

Bashar Barackah Jackson (Pop Smoke) (Musician)

Ja'net DuBois (Actor)

Andrew Weatherall (Music producer)

Harry Gregg (Soccer star)

Jason Davis (Actor)

Caroline Flack (TV presenter)

Esther Scott (Actor)

Lindsey Lagestee (Musician)

John Shrapnel (Actor)

Lynn Cohen (Actor)

Raphaël Coleman (Actor)

Orson Bean (Actor)

Kirk Douglas (Actor)

Danny Ayres (Speedway racer)

Andy Gill (Musician)

Nicholas Parsons (Broadcaster)

Jack Burns (Actor)

Terry Jones (Actor)

Derek Fowlds (Actor)

Therese Dion (TV star)

Christopher Tolkien (Author)

Rocky Johnson (Wrestler)

Stan Kirsch (Actor)

Edd Byrnes (Actor)

Neil Peart (Musician)

Silvio Horta (Script writer)

Stephen Clements (Presenter)

Christopher Beeny (Actor)

Derek Acorah (Actor)

Nathael Julan (Soccer star)

Chris Barker (Soccer star)

Lexii Alijai (Musician)

IN MEMORIAM

Ruth Bader Ginsburg (1933-2020)

Ruth Bader Gainsburg was only the second female to serve on the USA Supreme Court. The iconic Justice will be remembered as a liberal advocate for gender equality and women's rights, among her plethora of accomplishments. Dubbed 'The Notorious R.B.G', Ginsburg was named among Time Magazine's (2005) 100 Most Influential people. Among her notable awards are honorary Doctor of Laws by Willamette University (2009), Princeton University (2010) and Harvard University (2011). Ginsburg died at her home in Washington DC on September 18th, 2020, after a long struggle with metastatic pancreatic cancer. According to her granddaughter, Ginsburg's dying wish was to be replaced after the November 3rd presidential elections, but President Trump swiftly nominated Amy Coney Barret who is expected to be confirmed as a replacement.

> REAL CHANGE,
> ENDURING CHANGE,
> HAPPENS ONE
> STEP AT A TIME.
>
> - Ruth Bader Ginsburg

Chadwick Aaron Boseman (1976-2020)

Chadwick Aaron Boseman was an American actor, educated at Howard University. Boseman's breakthrough performance came as baseball player Jackie Robinson in the biographical film 42 (2013). He continued to portray historical figures, starring in Get on up (2014) as singer James Brown and Marshall (2017) as Supreme Court Justice Thurgood Marshall. It was his portrayal of the superhero Black Panther in the Marvel Cinematic Universe films Captain America: Civil War, Black Panther, Avengers: Infinity War and Avengers: Endgame that earned him global fame as an iconic Black actor. On August 28th, 2020, Boseman died of colon cancer, a condition he had kept private, while he worked on many of the aforenamed films.

> WHEN I STAND BEFORE GOD AT THE END
> OF MY LIFE, I WOULD HOPE THAT I WOULD
> NOT HAVE A SINGLE BIT OF TALENT LEFT,
> AND COULD SAY, 'I USED EVERYTHING YOU GAVE ME
>
> - Chadwick Boseman

Kobe Bean Byant (1978-2020)

The world of sport was shaken by the news of the sudden death of Kobe Bryant and seven other people, including his thirteen-year-old daughter Gianna and the pilot, in a helicopter crash, thirty miles from downtown LA, in California, on January 26th, 2020. Bryant was one of the most popular basketball players in Los Angeles, and across the globe. In addition to the basketball legacy, Bryant, the youngest of three and only son was a multilingual (fluent in English, Italian and Spanish) practicing Catholic who attributed his faith to surviving difficult phases in his life. Bryant had musical talents that saw him released his first single K.O.B.E in January 2000. In 2018 Bryant wrote, produced, and hosted the television series, Detail, that intellectualised the game of basketball. Together with his wife, Bryant founded the Kobe and Vanessa Bryant Family Foundation whose goal is to help young people in need. He also made a substantive founding donation to the National Museum of African American History and Culture, in Washington DC.

> EVERYTHING NEGATIVE -
> PRESSURE, CHALLENGES -
> IS ALL AN OPPORTUNITY FOR ME TO RISE.
>
> - Kobe Bryant

References:

https://www.bbc.co.uk/news/business-52319575

https://www.cnbc.com/2020/05/14/dubai-airports-passenger-numbers-plunged-20percent-in-the-first-quarter-as-coronavirus-crushed-travel.html

https://adamstart.com/covid-19-challenge-winners/

https://www.rnz.co.nz/news/national/413584/air-traffic-plummets-by-85-percent

https://www.fitchratings.com/research/sovereigns/coronavirus-macro-policy-responses-unprecedented-03-06-2020

https://www.childrenscommissioner.gov.uk/2020/06/11/the-numbers-behind-homeschooling-during-lockdown/

(https://www.telegraph.co.uk/education-and-careers/2020/06/02/gsce-year-kids-risk-forgotten-generation/).

https://news.sky.com/story/liverpool-beat-tottenham-to-win-champions-league-final-11733110

https://www.ft.com/content/be9c5a5e-1280-4281-8b28-04717d2c7e66

https://en.wikipedia.org/wiki/Katr%C3%ADn_Jakobsd%C3%B3ttir

https://www.theguardian.com/uk-news/2020/apr/03/uk-road-travel-falls-to-1955-levels-as-covid-19-lockdown-takes-hold-coronavirus-traffic

https://www.theguardian.com/world/2020/apr/13/atlanta-hartsfield-jackson-coronavirus-airport-shut-down

https://www.kcl.ac.uk/news/how-coronavirus-is-impacting-london

https://www.mirror.co.uk/3am/celebrity-news/celebrity-deaths-2020-famous-faces-21200495

Naomi Watasa Lumutenga | Author

Naomi Watasa Lumutenga is a Ugandan-born retired teacher who lives in Maidstone, Kent, United Kingdom. She is an alumna of Makerere University (Uganda), University College London and a researcher at Canterbury Christ Church University. After many years of teaching Geography and Economics and holding various administrative and advisory positions, she co-founded Higher Education Resource Services-East Africa, an organisation that trains women in leadership and administration, in African countries. She is an established motivational speaker, a researcher, a passionate social justice activist and continues to engage with local, national, and global issues.

Taaya Marjorie Griffith | Illustrator

Taaya Marjorie Griffith is an accomplished illustrator based in Thurrock, Essex, United Kingdom. She studied a Design degree at Kingston University (Surrey) and is the founder and executive director of Swanky Portraits; a business that focuses on illustrated, personalised books and other merchandise. She is passionate about giving back to the community, a philosophy that underpins her professional work and hobbies.

Other books by this author & illustrator

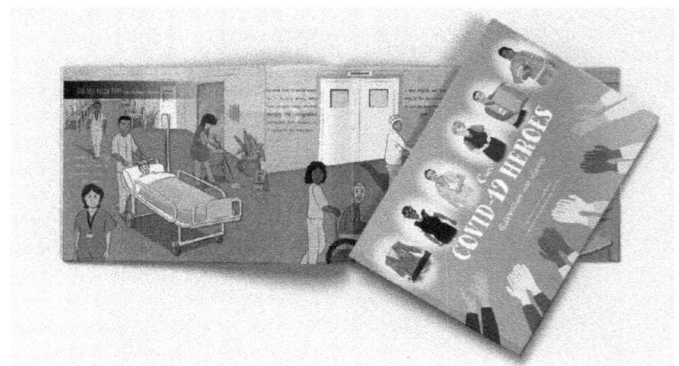

OUR COVID-19 HEROES | Published 2020